Alpha

Published in North America by Alpha North America, 1635 Emerson Lane, Naperville, IL 60540

© 2016 Alpha International, Holy Trinity Brompton, Brompton Road, London SW7 1JA, UK

Alpha Guide

This edition first printed by Alpha North America in 2008

Printed in the United States of America

Unless otherwise noted, all Scripture in this publication is from the Holy Bible, New International Version (NIV), Copyright 1973, 1978, 1984, 2011 International Bible Society, used by permission of Zondervan. All rights reserved. *Holy Bible*, New Living Translation, copyright ©1996, 2004, 2015 by Tyndale House Foundation. Used by permission of Tyndale House Publishers, Inc., Carol Stream, Illinois 60188. All rights reserved. The New Testament in Modern English by J. B. Phillips copyright ©1960, 1972 J. B. Phillips. Administered by The Archbishops' Council of the Church of England. Used by permission. *Good News Translation (GNT)* Copyright ©1992 by American Bible Society.

ISBN 978 1 938328 82 4

7 8 9 10 Printing/Year 20 19 18 17

Contents

WELCOME TO ALPHA – A SERIES OF INTERACTIVE SESSIONS TO DISCUSS LIFE AND THE CHRISTIAN FAITH IN AN INFORMAL, FUN AND FRIENDLY ENVIRONMENT.

This guide outlines the content of the fifteen talks, which each look at a different aspect of the Christian faith. After each talk, there is a time for discussion in small groups—a place where you can ask questions, delve into different issues and find out what others think.

This is your guide, so use it however you like. Write, scribble, note, jot, or doodle. Whatever helps.

My notes:

Is there
more to
life
than

this

What, if any, has been your experience of Christianity?
- **Boring?**
- **Untrue?**
- **Irrelevant?**

At the heart of the Christian faith is the person of Jesus Christ.
Then Jesus declared, "I am the bread of life." (John 6:35)

1. JESUS SAID, "I AM THE WAY."

The first-order questions of life:
- Is there more to life than this?
- What am I doing on earth?
- What is the point of life?
- What is the purpose of my life?
- Where am I heading?

C. S. Lewis: "I believe in Christianity as I believe that the sun has risen: not only because I see it, but because by it I see everything else."[1]

Jesus is the lens through which we see God. He is the way to God.

Jesus is also the lens by which we see the world in a totally different dimension and clarity.

2. JESUS SAID, "I AM THE TRUTH."

C. S. Lewis: "Christianity, if false, is of no importance, and if true, of infinite importance. The only thing it cannot be is moderately important."[2]

- Truth—understood intellectually (head knowledge)
- Truth—experienced as a relationship (heart knowledge)

3. JESUS SAID, "I AM THE LIFE."

"I have come that [you] may have life, and have it to the full." (John 10:10)

Jesus came to deal with:
- The things that spoil our lives
- Our guilt

God loves you and He came, in the person of His Son, Jesus, to set you free to enjoy life to the full.

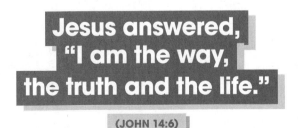

Jesus answered, "I am the way, the truth and the life."

(JOHN 14:6)

9

RECOMMENDED READING

What's So Amazing About Grace?
Philip Yancey

The Return of the Prodigal Son: A Story of Homecoming
Henri J. M. Nouwen

Does Religion Do More Harm Than Good?
Nicky Gumbel

Who is
Jesus

Did Jesus exist?
- Evidence outside the New Testament about Jesus includes:
  - Tacitus and Suetonius, Roman historians
  - Josephus, Jewish historian
- Evidence within the New Testament

How do we know that what was written down in the New Testament has not been changed over the years?

ANCIENT WRITINGS

Key

Time lapse ▬▬▬▬ = 200 years ● Number of copies found

Original work first written

30–310 years

NEW TESTAMENT
Copies found:

5,000+ Greek

10,000 Latin

9,300 Other languages

WORK	WRITTEN	EARLIEST COPY	TIME LAPSE	COPIES
HERODOTUS	488–428 BC	AD 900	1,300 years	8
THUCYDIDES	c. 460–400 BC	c. AD 900	1,300 years	8
TACITUS	AD 100	AD 1100	1,000 years	20
CAESAR'S GALLIC WAR	58–50 BC	AD 900	950 years	9–10
LIVY'S ROMAN HISTORY	59 BC–AD 17	AD 900	900 years	20
NEW TESTAMENT	AD 40–100	AD 130 (full manuscripts AD 350)	30–310 years	5,000 + Greek 10,000 Latin 9,300 others

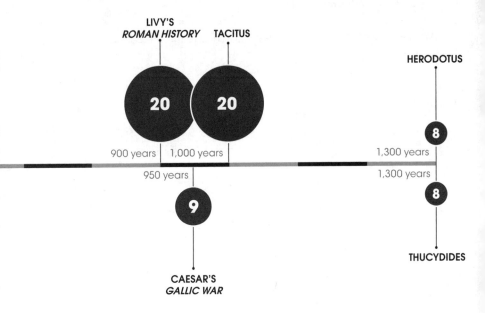

LIVY'S ROMAN HISTORY

TACITUS

HERODOTUS

20   20

900 years | 1,000 years

1,300 years

8

950 years

1,300 years

9

8

CAESAR'S GALLIC WAR

THUCYDIDES

Was Jesus fully human?
- He had a human body.
  - tired (John 4:6)
  - hungry (Matthew 4:2)

- He had human emotions.
  - anger (Mark 11:15–17)
  - love (Mark 10:21)
  - sadness (John 11:32–36)

- He had human experiences.
  - temptation (Mark 1:13)
  - learning (Luke 2:46–52)
  - work (Mark 6:3)
  - obedience (Luke 2:51)

Was He more than a man, a great human, a religious teacher?
(Matthew 16:13–16)

1. WHAT DID HE SAY ABOUT HIMSELF?

• **Teaching centered on himself**
  - "I am the bread of life." (John 6:35)
  - "If the Son sets you free, you are truly free." (John 8:36, NLT)
  - "I am the light of the world." (John 8:12)
  - "I am the way and the truth and the life." (John 14:6)
  - "Come to me...." (Matthew 11:28–29)
  - Receive me—receive God. (Matthew 10:40)
  - Welcome me—welcome God. (Mark 9:37)
  - "Anyone who has seen me has seen the Father." (John 14:9)

• **His indirect claims**
  - To forgive sins (Mark 2:5)
  - To judge the world (Matthew 25:31, 32, 40, 45)

• **His direct claims**
  - Messiah (Mark 14:61–62)
  - Son of God (Mark 14:61)
  - God the Son (John 20:26–29)
  - "I and the Father are one." (John 10:30)

Author of *The Chronicles of Narnia* and Oxford historian C. S. Lewis wrote:

"A man who was merely a man and said the sort of things Jesus said would not be a great moral teacher. He would either be (insane)... or else he would be 'the Devil of Hell.' You must make your choice. Either this man was, and is, the Son of God, or else (insane) or something worse... but let us not come up with any patronizing nonsense about his being a great human teacher. He has not left that open to us. He did not intend to."[3]

2. WHAT EVIDENCE IS THERE TO SUPPORT HIS CLAIMS?

- His teaching (Mark 12:31; Luke 6:31; Matthew 5:44)
- His life/works (John 2:1–11; 10:37–38)
- His character (Luke 23:34)
- His fulfilment of Old Testament prophecy
- His conquest of death

Evidence for the resurrection:

- **His absence from the tomb**
  - Theories:
    Jesus did not die (John 19:33–34)
    Disciples stole the body
    Authorities stole the body
    Robbers stole the body (John 20:1–9)

- **His presence with the disciples**
  - Did they hallucinate?
  - Number of appearances over a six-week period
    11+ appearances
    500+ people
  - Nature of appearances (Luke 24:36–43)

- **Immediate effect**
  - Birth and growth of Christian church

- **Effect down the ages**
  - Experience of Christians down the ages
  - Over 2,300 million Christians in the world today

RECOMMENDED READING

Mere Christianity
C. S. Lewis

The Case for Christ
Lee Strobel

Orthodoxy
G. K. Chesterton

Jesus Is
Judah Smith

Session 3

Why did Jesus die

Why is the cross the symbol of Christianity?

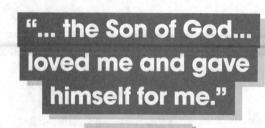

"... the Son of God... loved me and gave himself for me."

(GALATIANS 2:20)

1. THE PROBLEM

"All have sinned and fall short of the glory of God." (Romans 3:23).

- **Pollution** of sin (Mark 7:20–23)
- **Power** of sin (John 8:34)
- **Penalty** for sin (Romans 6:23)
- **Partition** of sin (Isaiah 59:2)

2. THE SOLUTION

- "The self-substitution of God" (1 Peter 2:24)
- Agony of the cross (Isaiah 53:6)

3. THE RESULT

The cross shows:
- You are infinitely valuable to God.
- Jesus is the supreme example of love. (John 15:13)
- God is not aloof from suffering.
- The powers of evil have been defeated: the resurrection wasn't the reversal of a defeat; it was the manifestation of a victory.

- The **partition** has been removed (2 Corinthians 5:19)
  - Reconciliation with God and in other relationships

- The **penalty** has been paid
  - Justified ("Just-as-if-I'd never sinned")

- The **power** of sin has been broken
  - "If the Son sets you free, you are truly free." (John 8:36, NLT)

- The **pollution** has been removed
  - "… the blood of Jesus, … purifies us from all sin." (1 John 1:7)
  - When you are forgiven, you want to forgive.

RECOMMENDED READING

The Cross of Christ
John Stott

Why Does God Allow Suffering?
Nicky Gumbel

Unreachable
Darrell Tunningley

Mud, Sweat and Tears
Bear Grylls

Why Jesus?
Nicky Gumbel

The Hiding Place
Corrie Ten Boom

How can I have faith

"This means that anyone who belongs to Christ has become a new person. The old life is gone; a new life has begun!"
(2 Corinthians 5:17, NLT)

A Christian is a Christ-ian: someone who follows and puts their faith in Jesus Christ.

How that happens varies enormously. For some there is a definite moment; for others it is a more gradual process.

• When you receive Christ, you become a child of God. (John 1:12)
• God wants you to be sure of your faith.

"I write these things to you who believe in the name of the Son of God so that you may know that you have eternal life."

(1 JOHN 5:13)

Faith is not a blind leap, but a step based on evidence.

1. THE WORD OF GOD

We must not only trust our feelings, which can be changeable and may even be deceptive at times, but instead rely on God's promises.

- "… faith comes from hearing the message, and the message is heard through the word about Christ." (Romans 10:17)
- "I will come in." (Revelation 3:20)
- "I am with you always." (Matthew 28:20)
- "I give them eternal life." (John 10:28)

2. THE WORK OF JESUS

You come exactly as you are. It's not about what you do or what you can achieve; it's about what has been done for you by Jesus on the cross.

- Free gift of God (Romans 6:23).
- It's free but not cheap: it cost Jesus His life.
- We receive it through repentance (turning away from sin) and faith (trust).

3. THE WITNESS OF THE HOLY SPIRIT

When someone becomes a Christian, God comes to live inside them by His Holy Spirit (Romans 8:9).

- He transforms us from within.
  - Our characters (Galatians 5:22–23)
  - Our relationships

- He brings a deep personal conviction that we are God's children.
  - Faith to knowledge (Romans 8:15–16)

Here is a very simple prayer that you can pray to open the door of your heart to Jesus Christ and invite Him to come into your life by His Spirit:

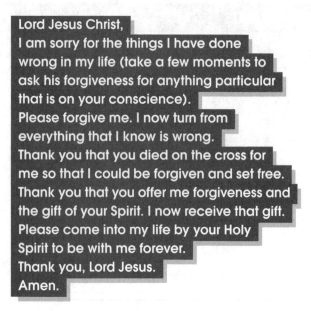

Lord Jesus Christ,
I am sorry for the things I have done wrong in my life (take a few moments to ask his forgiveness for anything particular that is on your conscience).
Please forgive me. I now turn from everything that I know is wrong.
Thank you that you died on the cross for me so that I could be forgiven and set free.
Thank you that you offer me forgiveness and the gift of your Spirit. I now receive that gift.
Please come into my life by your Holy Spirit to be with me forever.
Thank you, Lord Jesus.
Amen.

RECOMMENDED READING

The Reason for God
Tim Keller

Is Faith Irrational?
Nicky Gumbel

One Step Beyond: One Man's Journey From Near Death to New Life
Gram Seed

Session 5

pray

**Why and
how do I**

1. WHAT IS CHRISTIAN PRAYER?

Prayer is the most important activity of our lives.

"For through [Jesus] we both have access to the Father by one Spirit."
(Ephesians 2:18)

• **To the Father**
  – "… to your father" (Matthew 6:6)
  – "… in heaven" (v.9)
• **Through the Son**
  – "I have called you friends" (John 15:15)
• **By the Spirit**
  – "… the Spirit helps us" (Romans 8:26)

2. WHY PRAY?

• Develops a relationship with God
• Rewards of prayer (Matthew 6:6)
  – Presence of God
  – Peace (Philippians 4:6–7)
  – Perspective
  – Power
• Results of prayer (Matthew 7:7–11)

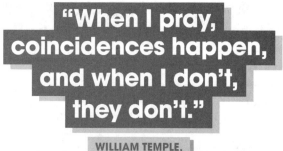

"When I pray, coincidences happen, and when I don't, they don't."

**WILLIAM TEMPLE,
THE FORMER ARCHBISHOP OF CANTERBURY**

3. DOES GOD ALWAYS ANSWER PRAYER?

- Yes—you receive what you prayed for, sometimes immediately.
- No—sometimes an obvious reason why not; other times we may not understand straight away why the answer is no.
- Wait—for the right timing.

4. HOW DO WE PRAY?

- **Thank you**—count your blessings, not your problems.
- **Sorry**—confess your sins (John 13:6–10).
- **Please**—"Give us today our daily bread." (Matthew 6:11): ask for anything you need.

5. WHEN SHOULD WE PRAY?

- **Anywhere, anytime**
  - (Ephesians 6:18)
- **Alone (Matthew 6:6)**
  - Regular pattern
  - Best part of the day (Mark 1:35)
- **With others**
  - There's power in praying together
  - "Again, truly I tell you that if two of you on earth agree about any-thing they ask for, it will be done for them by my Father in heaven." (Matthew 18:19)

Three simple tips:
- Keep it real
- Keep it simple
- Keep it going

RECOMMENDED READING

God on Mute
Pete Greig

Too Busy Not to Pray
Bill Hybels

What About Other Religions?
Nicky Gumbel

Session 6

Why and
how should
I read
the Bible

The Bible is the most...
• Popular
• Powerful
• Precious (Psalm 19:10)
... book in the world.

"Man shall not live on bread alone, but on every **word** that comes from the mouth of God." (Matthew 4:4).

1. BRINGING REVELATION - GOD HAS SPOKEN

• Bible: collection of books by 40+ authors over 1600 years
• Inspired: God-breathed

"All Scripture is God-breathed and is useful for teaching, rebuking, correcting and training in righteousness." (2 Timothy 3:16)

But what about difficulties in the Bible?
• Jesus is the interpretive key
• It's authoritative (2 Timothy 3:16–17)
• Practical wisdom:
  – Guidelines for living
  – Guidance for good decisions

2. BUILDING RELATIONSHIP - GOD SPEAKS

The Bible is like a love letter from God:
- To those exploring faith (Romans 10:17, John 20:31)
- To those who are Christians
  - Become like Jesus (2 Corinthians 3:18)
  - Joy and peace in the midst of a storm (Psalm 23:5)
  - Guidance (Psalm 119:105)
  - Health/healing (Proverbs 4:20–22)
  - Defense against spiritual attack (Matthew 4:1–11)
  - Power (Hebrews 4:12)
  - Cleansing (John 15:3)

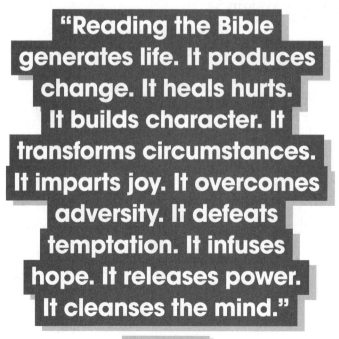

"Reading the Bible generates life. It produces change. It heals hurts. It builds character. It transforms circumstances. It imparts joy. It overcomes adversity. It defeats temptation. It infuses hope. It releases power. It cleanses the mind."

RICK WARREN

3. HOW CAN WE HEAR GOD SPEAK THROUGH THE BIBLE

- Make a plan
  - Find a time
  - Find a place ("a solitary place," Mark 1:35)

- Find a pattern
  - Ask God to speak:
  Read a short passage
  Bible reading notes
  Bible in One Year app – bibleinoneyear.org

  - Ask yourself:
  What does it say to me?
  What does it mean to me?
  How does it apply to me?

- Respond in prayer
- Put it into practice (Matthew 7:24)

RECOMMENDED READING

Why Trust the Bible?
Amy Orr-Ewing

30 Days
Nicky Gumbel

The Bible (*The Message* is an acceptable paraphrase)

NIV Alpha Bible in One Year

Read the daily Bible in One Year commentary by Nicky Gumbel at **bibleinoneyear.org** or download the app from the App Store.

Session 7

How does God guide us

"For we are God's masterpiece. He has created us anew in Christ Jesus, so we can do the good things he planned for us long ago.'" (Ephesians 2:10, NLT)

Why involve God in the decisions we make?

- God promises to guide us.
  - (Psalm 32:8)
  - (John 10:3–4, 27)

- God has a good plan for our lives.
  - (Jeremiah 29:11)
  - (Romans 12:2)
  - (John 10:10, 15)

How does God guide us?

1. COMMANDING SCRIPTURE

- General will
  - General instruction for marriage, work, money, children, elderly relatives (2 Timothy 3:16; Psalm 119:105, 130–133)

- Primary calling
  - To love God
  - To love others
  - To become like Jesus

2. COMPELLING SPIRIT

- God speaks as you pray (Acts 13:1–3)

- Strong desire to do something
  - "It is God who works in you to will and to act in order to fulfill his good purpose." (Philippians 2:13)

- Sometimes He guides in more unusual ways
  - Prophecy, for example, Agabus (Acts 11:27–28; 21:10–11)
  - Dreams (Matthew 1:20)
  - Visions/pictures (Acts 16:10)
  - Angels (Genesis 18; Matthew 2:19; Acts 12:7)
  - Audible voice (1 Samuel 3:4–14)

3. COUNSEL OF THE SAINTS

- "… the wise listen to advice." (Proverbs 12:15)

- "Plans are established by seeking advice." (Proverbs 20:18)

- Need for testing (1 John 4:1)
  - Is it in line with the Bible?
  - Is it loving? (1 John 4:16)
  - Is it strengthening, encouraging and comforting?
    (1 Corinthians 14:3)
  - Does it bring the peace of God? (Colossians 3:15)

Ultimately, we are responsible for our decisions, but it is a blessing to have others to talk to about the decisions we are making.

4. COMMON SENSE

- "Reflect on what I am saying, for the Lord will give you insight into all this." (2 Timothy 2:7)

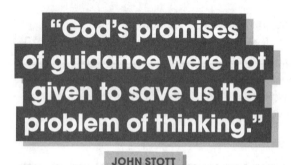

> "God's promises of guidance were not given to save us the problem of thinking."
>
> JOHN STOTT

5. CIRCUMSTANTIAL SIGNS

- "And we know that in all things God works for the good of those who love him, who have been called according to his purpose." (Romans 8:28)
- "In their hearts humans plan their course, but the Lord establishes their steps." (Proverbs 16:9; Psalm 37:5)
- Sometimes God closes doors. (Acts 16:7)
- Sometimes God opens doors. (1 Corinthians 16:9)
- Sometimes we need to persevere despite the circumstances and trust God.
- Be patient.
- We all make mistakes—God forgives. (Joel 2:25)

RECOMMENDED READING

Chasing the Dragon
Jackie Pullinger

Session 8

Who
is the **Holy Spirit**

For a long time in the church the person and work of the Holy Spirit has been:

- Ignored
  - Sometimes a greater concentration on the Father and the Son, but the Holy Spirit is biblical and third person of the Trinity.
- Misunderstood
  - "Holy Ghost" sounds like an impersonal force. But the Holy Spirit is a person, not an "it."
- Resisted
  - Fear of what He does, but the Holy Spirit is gentle.

1. HE WAS INVOLVED IN CREATION

- Bringing order out of chaos (Genesis 1:1–2)
- The Creator Spirit—giving life to mankind (Genesis 2:7)

2. HE CAME UPON PARTICULAR PEOPLE AT PARTICULAR TIMES FOR PARTICULAR TASKS

- Bezalel—for artistic work (Exodus 31:1–5)
- Gideon—for leadership (Judges 6:14–15, 34)
- Samson—for strength and power (Judges 15:14)
- Isaiah—for prophecy (Isaiah 61:1–3)

3. HE WAS PROMISED BY THE FATHER

- The promise of a "new thing"
  - "I will put my Spirit in you." (Ezekiel 36:26–27)
  - "I will remove from you your heart of stone and give you a heart of flesh." (Ezekiel 36:26–27)
  - "I will pour out my Spirit on all people." (Joel 2:28–29)

However, the prophecies remained unfulfilled for at least 300 years.

With the coming of Jesus there is a great activity of the Spirit—not just for particular people at particular times but for everyone.

- Everyone surrounding the birth of Jesus is filled with the Holy Spirit:
  - Mary (Luke 1:35)
  - Elizabeth (Luke 1:41)
  - John the Baptist (Luke 3:16)

4. JOHN THE BAPTIST LINKS HIM WITH JESUS

"John answered them all, 'I baptize you with water. But one more powerful than I will come, the straps of whose sandals I am not worthy to untie. He will baptize you with the Holy Spirit and with fire.'" (Luke 3:16)

- Jesus was filled with the Spirit
  - Jesus received power through the anointing of the Holy Spirit at His baptism. (Luke 3:22; Luke 4:1,14,18)

5. JESUS PREDICTS HIS PRESENCE (John 7:37–39)

However, He tells them to wait for the gift promised by the Father (Acts 1:4–5,8; Luke 24:49).

- At Pentecost the disciples were filled with the Spirit and received:
  - New languages (Acts 2:4–12)
  - New boldness (Acts 2:14)
  - New power (Acts 2:37–41)

We live in the age of the Spirit. God has promised to give His Spirit to every Christian (Acts 2:37–39).

"Whoever believes in me, as the Scripture has said, will have streams of living water flowing from within."

(JOHN 7:37-38)

RECOMMENDED READING

Come, Creator Spirit
Raniero Cantalamessa

Session 9

What
does the
Holy Spirit do

- New birth (John 3:3–8)
- Born into a family

1. SONS AND DAUGHTERS OF GOD

- Adoption (Romans 8:14–17)
  - Highest privilege (v.14)
  - Closest intimacy (v.15)
  - Deepest experience (v.16)

2. DEVELOPING THE RELATIONSHIP

"For through him we both have access to the Father by one Spirit."
(Ephesians 2:18)

- He helps us to pray. (Romans 8:26)
- He enables us to understand God's Word. (Ephesians 1:17–18)

3. THE FAMILY LIKENESS

- He makes us more like Jesus. (2 Corinthians 3:18)
- Fruit of the Spirit (Galatians 5:22–23)

4. UNITY IN THE FAMILY

- (Ephesians 4:3–6)

5. GIFTS FOR ALL THE CHILDREN

- The Holy Spirit gives everybody gifts for the common good.
  (1 Corinthians 12:4–11)

6. A GROWING FAMILY

- The Spirit of God gives us power.
  - To be witnesses for Christ (Acts 1:8)
  - For service (Acts 1:8)

"The Spirit and the bride say, 'Come!' And let the one who hears say, 'Come!' Let the one who is thirsty come; let the one who wishes take the free gift of the water of life." (Revelation 22:17)

....

....

....

....

....

....

....

....

....

....

....

....

RECOMMENDED READING

Lifechange
Ed. Mark Elsdon-Dew

The God Who Changes Lives 1, 2, 3 & 4
Ed. M. Elsdon-Dew

How
can I be filled
with the
Holy Spirit

What the Holy Spirit does and brings to our lives is all about love.

Every Christian has the Holy Spirit (Romans 8:9) but not every Christian is filled with the Spirit.

Five categories of people:

1. Longing (Pentecost—Acts 2:2–4)
2. Receptive (Samaria—Acts 8:14–23)
3. Hostile (Paul—Acts 8:1, 3; 9:1–2)
4. Uninformed (Ephesus—Acts 19:1–6)
5. Unlikely (Gentiles—Acts 10:44–47)

What happened to Cornelius and his household when the Spirit came upon them? (Acts 10:44–46)

1. THEY EXPERIENCED THE LOVE OF GOD

"... the Holy Spirit came on all who heard the message.... Then Peter said ... 'they have received the Holy Spirit just as we have.'" (Acts 10:44–47)

- There were physical manifestations.
- Everyone's experience is different.
- What matters is God's love being poured out into your heart. (Romans 5:5)
- Pursue the Person, not the experience. (Ephesians 3:14–19)

2. THEY EXPRESSED THEIR LOVE FOR GOD

"For they heard them ... praising God." (Acts 10:46)

- Fear of emotion: emotion versus emotionalism
  - Emotion is an important part of faith and love for God.
  - Express with our whole bodies: raised hands; a traditional form of prayer.

3. THEY RECEIVED A NEW LOVE LANGUAGE

"For they heard them speaking in tongues." (Acts 10:46)

- Not all Christians speak in tongues
  - Not the mark of being a Christian.
  - Not necessarily a mark of being filled with the Spirit.
  - There are no first- or second-class Christians.
  - It is not the most important gift.

- What is the gift of tongues?
  - Human or angelic language (1 Corinthians 13:1)
  - A form of prayer (1 Corinthians 14:2)
  - Builds up the individual
  - Transcends the language barrier (1 Corinthians 14:14)
  - The speaker is in full control.
  - Public use requires an interpretation.

- Why is it helpful?
  - Worship (1 Corinthians 14:15)
  - Praying for oneself (1 Corinthians 14:2,4)
  - Praying for others

- Why ask for the gift of tongues?
  - Paul encourages its use (1 Corinthians 14:5,18,39)

What are the barriers to being filled with the Holy Spirit?

- Doubt: "I don't think I will receive."
- Fear: "What will happen to me?"
- Inadequacy: "I'm not good enough."

But Jesus says:

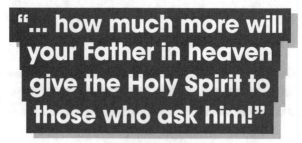

"... how much more will your Father in heaven give the Holy Spirit to those who ask him!"

(LUKE 11:13)

RECOMMENDED READING

The Mystery of Pentecost
Raniero Cantalamessa

Sober Intoxication of the Spirit: Filled with the Fullness of God
Raniero Cantalamessa

How can I make the most of the rest of my

life

1. WHAT SHOULD WE DO?

- Break with the past
  - "Do not conform to the pattern of this world." (Romans 12:2)
  - "Don't let the world around you squeeze you into its mould." (v.2, J. B. Phillips)

- Make a new start
  - "Let God transform you inwardly by a complete change." (v.2, GNT)

- God has treasures in store for us.
  - Sincere love (v.9)
  - Enthusiasm in your relationship with God (Romans v.11)

2. HOW DO WE DO IT?

- "Offer your bodies ...." (Romans 12:1)
  - Time
  - Priorities
  - Ambitions (Matthew 6:33)
  - Money
  - Ears
  - Eyes
  - Mouth
  - Hands
  - Sexuality

- "... as a living sacrifice."
  - We will find freedom.
  - There will be a cost.
  - There will be challenges.

3. WHY SHOULD WE DO IT?

• What God has done for us?
  – "… in view of God's mercy." (Romans 12:1)

• What God has planned for our future?
  – "… his good, pleasing and perfect will." (v.2)

RECOMMENDED READING

The Jesus Lifestyle
Nicky Gumbel

Life in Christ
Raniero Cantalamessa

How can I resist

evil

Where does evil come from?

* Triple alliance:
    – World—the enemy around
    – Flesh—the enemy within
    – Devil—the enemy above

1. WHY SHOULD WE BELIEVE THAT THE DEVIL EXISTS?
(Romans 12:21)

* Scripture: The Bible presents a personal, spiritual being in active rebellion against God.
    – Old Testament (Isaiah 14; Job 1; 1 Chronicles 21:1)
    – Jesus (Luke 10:17–20)
    – Peter (1 Peter 5:8–11)
    – Paul (Ephesians 6:11–12)

* Tradition: Christians down through the ages have believed.

* Reason: It makes sense of the world we see around us.
    – Why do bad things happen?

Avoid two extremes: Disbelief vs unhealthy, excessive interest

2. WHAT ARE THE DEVIL'S TACTICS? (Genesis 3)

- The devil wants to destroy our lives. (John 10:10)
  - Doubt (Genesis 3:1, Matthew 4:3)
  - Temptation (Genesis 2:16–17)
  - Deception (Genesis 3:4)
  - Condemnation creates doubt

But, "there is… no condemnation for those who are in Christ Jesus." (Romans 8:1)

3. WHAT IS OUR POSITION? (Colossians 1:13)

- We are transferred from the dominion of darkness to the kingdom of Jesus.
- We experience God's love.
- It's a process—we won't be complete until Jesus returns.

4. HOW DO WE DEFEND OURSELVES? (Ephesians 6)

"Be strong in the Lord…. Put on the full armor of God, so that you can take your stand against the devil's schemes." (Ephesians 6:10–11)

1 **Focus on Jesus – belt of truth (v.14)**
- "I am the truth." (John 14:6)
- Authenticity, integrity, openness in your life

Keep your relationships right –
breastplate of righteousness (v.14) **2**
- Keep short accounts with God
- Ask forgiveness from God and others

3 **Get involved in service –**
boots of the gospel of peace (v.15)
- The readiness to speak of Christ (Isaiah 52:7–10)

Trust God in difficult times –
shield of faith (v.16) **4**
- The devil will challenge us with
  doubt, fear, anxiety, lust…
- Keep trusting; don't give up on your faith

5 **Win the battle of the mind –**
helmet of salvation (v.17)
- Salvation = freedom
- Protect your mind: temptation starts
  with a thought, which leads to action

Know your Bible –
sword of the Spirit (v.17) **6**
- Soak yourself in the Word of God
- The only offensive piece of armor (Hebrews 4:12)

5. HOW DO WE ATTACK?

- Prayer: "Pray in the Spirit on all occasions...." (Ephesians 6:18)

- Action: "Do not be overcome by evil, but overcome evil with good." (Romans 12:21)

RECOMMENDED READING

The Screwtape Letters
C. S. Lewis

Café Theology
Michael Lloyd

....

....

....

....

....

....

....

....

....

....

....

....

....

....

....

....

....

....

....

....

Why and how should I tell others

"Go and make disciples of all nations, baptizing them in the name of the Father and of the Son and of the Holy Spirit, and teaching them to obey everything I have commanded you." (Matthew 28:18–20)

Why tell others?
- Jesus told us to
- For the needs of others – spiritual hunger in the world
- It's good news: "Gospel" = Good News
- Two opposite dangers
  - Insensitivity
  - Fear

How do we tell others?

1. PRESENCE (Matthew 5:13–16)

- We are called to be salt and light. (vv.13–14)
- When people know we are Christians, they watch our lives. (v.16)

"You are the salt of the earth... You are the light of the world... let your light shine before others, that they may see your good deeds and glorify your Father in heaven." (Matthew 5:13–16)

2. PERSUASION (Matthew 5:13–16)

"Since ... we know what it is to fear the Lord, we try to persuade others."
(2 Corinthians 5:11)

- Work out the answers to common questions.
  - For example: "What about other religions?" and "How can a God of love allow suffering?"
- Do it with gentleness and respect. (1 Peter 3:15)

3. PROCLAMATION (John 1:39–46)

- We are not all called to be "evangelists" but we are all called to be "witnesses." (v.41)
- We can all say, "Come and see."

4. POWER (1 Thessalonians 1:5)

- The love of God poured into our hearts by the Holy Spirit.
- Healing

5. PRAYER (1 Thessalonians 1:5)

- For others
- For ourselves—to have boldness (Acts 4:29–31)

Don't give up—whenever you pass on the good news of Jesus, it has an effect. The gospel is the power of God. (Mark 4:15–20)

RECOMMENDED READING

The Case Against Christ
John Young

Searching Issues
Nicky Gumbel

APPENDIX

Suggestions for preparing your story

- **Make it short:**
  - Aim for three minutes—people switch off after that.

- **Make it personal:**
  - Don't preach—use "I" or "we," not "you."

- **Keep Christ central:**
  - They need to follow Him, not you.

- **The format:**
  - A little of your former life
  - How you came into your relationship with Christ
  - Something of what it has meant since then

- **Write it out in full:**
  - It's easier to edit your story when it's down on paper!

Session 14

Does God heal +oday

1. HEALING IN THE BIBLE

- Old Testament
  - I am the Lord who heals you. (Exodus 23:26)
  - The character of God—it's in His nature to heal.
  - Examples of God healing (2 Kings 5; Isaiah 38–39)

- The ministry of Jesus
  - "Jesus" means "Savior"
  - Greek "sozo" means "I save," also "I heal"
  - The healing miracles of Jesus form 25 percent of the Gospels
  - Jesus healed. (Matthew 4:23)
    He gave his followers authority to heal. (Luke 10:9, Acts)
    We see healing throughout church history.
    He commissions us to pray for and heal the sick today.

2. HEALING TODAY

- God heals explicably—through the medical profession.
- God heals inexplicably and directly.

> "When we prayed for no one, no one was healed. Now we pray for lots of people and some are healed."
>
> (JOHN WIMBER)

3. HOW DO WE HEAL?

- It's God who heals—not us.

- Simplicity—pray as Jesus did with love and compassion.
  (Matthew 9:36; Mark 1:41)

- Words of knowledge
  - Pictures
  - Sympathy pain
  - Impressions
  - Hear or see words

- Prayer—simple model
  - Where does it hurt?
  - Lay hands on the person.
  - Ask the Holy Spirit to come.
  - Ask how are they doing / if they can feel anything different.
  - Sometimes you need to pray more than once.

RECOMMENDED READING

Dancer Off Her Feet
Julie Sheldon

Power Evangelism
John Wimber

Session 15

What
about
the
church

What is the church?

- Popular misconceptions:
  - Church = services
  - Church = buildings

1. FRIENDS (John 15:15)

- Friends with Jesus
- Friends with one another (Hebrews 10:25)
- Greek word *koinonia* = fellowship

2. FAMILY (1 John 5:1)

- God as our Father (John 1:12)
- Brothers and sisters to each other (1 John 4:19 – 5:1)
- Importance of unity
- Jesus prayed "… that they may be one." (John 17:11)

Becoming a Christian involves:
- Something God does—He gives you the Holy Spirit
- Something you do—you repent and believe
- Something the church does—baptism

Baptism is the visible mark of being a member of the church.

Baptism signifies:
- Cleansing from sin (1 Corinthians 6:11)
- Dying and rising with Christ (Romans 6:3–5; Colossians 2:12)

3. HOME (Ephesians 2:19–22)

- Old Testament—physical temple was God's home
- New Testament—a building made up of people
  (Ephesians 2:21–22)
  - Jesus as the cornerstone (v.20)
  - Indwelt by God's Spirit (v.21) "a holy temple"
  - A place where people are loved, accepted, and welcomed home

4. JESUS (1 Corinthians 12:1–27)

- We are the body of Christ through whom the world will see Jesus.
  (v.27)
- Universal church (Ephesians 3:10,21; 5:23,25)
  - Unity (John 17:20–21)
  - Diversity (Ephesians 4:7–11)
  - Mutual dependence (vv.14–26)

5. LOVE (Ephesians 5:25–27, 32)

- Jesus loves the church; Jesus loves you. (v.25)
- The church should be famous for its love.

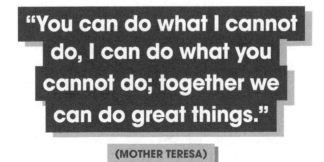

"You can do what I cannot do, I can do what you cannot do; together we can do great things."

(MOTHER TERESA)

RECOMMENDED READING

Questions of Life
Nicky Gumbel

ENDNOTES

1. C. S. Lewis, *The Weight of Glory* (Zondervan: Michigan, 2001)

2. *God in the Dock* by C. S. Lewis @ copyright C. S. Lewis Pte Ltd. 1970.

3. *Mere Christianity* by C. S. Lewis copyright © C. S. Lewis Pte. Ltd. 1942. Extract reprinted by permission.

4. Reprinted by permission of HarperCollins Publishers Ltd. © (1973) (J. B. Phillips).

A STEP OF FAITH

Excerpted from *Why Jesus?* by Nicky Gumbel

What Do We Have to Do?

The New Testament makes it clear that we have to do something to accept the gift that God offers. This is an act of faith. The disciple John writes, "God so loved the world that he gave his one and only Son, that whoever believes in him shall not perish but have eternal life." (John 3:16)

Believing involves an act of faith, based on all that we know about Jesus. It is not blind faith. It is putting our trust in a Person. In some ways it is like the step of faith taken by a bride and a bridegroom when they say "I will" on their wedding day.

The way people take this step of faith varies enormously, but I want to describe one way in which you can take this step of faith right now. It can be summarized by three very simple words:

"Sorry"

You have to ask God to forgive you for all the things you have done wrong and turn from everything that you know is wrong in your life. This is what the Bible means by "repentance."

"Thank You"

You believe that Jesus died for you on the cross. You need to thank Him for dying for you and for the offer of His free gifts of forgiveness, freedom, and His Spirit.

"Please"

God never forces His way into our lives. You need to accept His gift and invite Him to come and live within you by His Spirit.

If you would like to have a relationship with God and you are ready to say these three things, then here is a very simple prayer you can pray that will be the start of that relationship:

Lord Jesus Christ,

I am sorry for the things I have done wrong in my life.

(Take a few moments to ask His forgiveness for anything particular that is on your conscience.)

Please forgive me. I now turn from everything that I know is wrong.

Thank You that You died on the cross for me so that I could be forgiven and set free.

Thank You that You offer me forgiveness and the gift of Your Spirit. I now receive that gift.

Please come into my life by Your Holy Spirit, to be with me forever.

Thank you, Lord Jesus. Amen.

CONNECT WITH ALPHA

Let's connect

We welcome any opportunity to speak with you. Whether it's hearing your vision, or simply assisting you with a question, our team is waiting to talk with you.

alphausa.org/contact
800.362.5742

alphacanada.org/connect
800.743.0899

carribean.alpha.org/contact
868.671.0133

Tell us your story

Has your life been changed on Alpha? We would love to hear how God worked in your life. It might be just what someone considering attending Alpha needs to hear to take that next step.

Share your story:
USA: #MyAlphaStory
Canada: alphacanada.org/stories

Go deeper in the Word

Start your day with the Bible in One Year, a free Bible reading app with commentary by Nicky and Pippa Gumbel. Receive a daily email or audio commentary coordinated with the Bible in One Year reading plan.

alpha.org/bioy

Join our online communities

Looking for like-minded people who are talking about their recent experience on Alpha? Join the conversation on social media.

Find us on Facebook.
Twitter - @alphausa; @alphacanada; @alphalatam
Instagram - @alphausa | #RunAlpha

ALPHA RESOURCES

Why Jesus?   This booklet may be given to all participants at the start of Alpha. "The clearest, best illustrated and most challenging short presentation of Jesus that I know." – Michael Green

Why Christmas?   Why Easter?
The Christmas and Easter version of *Why Jesus?*

Questions of Life   Alpha in book form. In fifteen compelling chapters Nicky Gumbel points the way to an authentic Christianity which is exciting and relevant to the world today.

Searching Issues   The seven issues most often raised by participants on Alpha: suffering, other religions, does religion do more harm than good, is faith irrational, new spirituality, science and Christianity, and the Trinity.

The Jesus Lifestyle   Studies in the Sermon on the Mount showing how Jesus' teaching flies in the face of modern lifestyle and presents us with a radical alternative.

30 Days   Nicky Gumbel selects thirty passages from the Old and New Testament which can be read over thirty days. It is designed for those in Alpha and others who are interested in beginning to explore the Bible.

All titles are by Nicky Gumbel, Pioneer of Alpha

We hope you found this experience to be both challenging and enriching. If you would like more information about Alpha, please contact the following.

Alpha USA
1635 Emerson Lane
Naperville, IL 60540

800.362.5742
212.406.5269

info@alphausa.org
alphausa.org
alpharesources.org

@alphausa

Alpha in the Caribbean
Holy Trinity Brompton
Brompton Road
London SW7 1JA UK

+44 (0) 845.644.7544

americas@alpha.org
caribbean.Alpha.org

@AlphaCaribbean

Alpha Canada
Suite #230
11331 Coppersmith Way
Richmond, BC V7A 5J9

800.743.0899

office@alphacanada.org
alphacanada.org

Purchase resources in Canada:

Parasource
Canada
P.O. Box 98, 55 Woodslee Avenue
Paris, ON N3L 3E5

800.263.2664

custserv@parasource.com
parasource.com

NOTES

NOTES

NOTES